Bill,
To the true _outdoorsman_
in the family.
Merry Christmas '84

Love, Doug

ARCTIC
WILDLIFE

ARCTIC WILDLIFE

Monte Hummel

CHARTWELL
BOOKS, INC.

Published by
CHARTWELL BOOKS, INC.
A Division of **BOOK SALES, INC.**
110 Enterprise Avenue
Secaucus, New Jersey 07094

ISBN 0-89009-740-2

Produced by
Key Porter Books
70 The Esplanade
Toronto, Canada M5E 1R2

Designed by William Hindle

Typesetting by Imprint Typesetting, Toronto

Printed and bound in Italy by Sagdos S.p.A.

Page 1. The glaucous gull is one of the largest gulls in Canada. It breeds and nests only in the Arctic, along the coast of the mainland and islands, but rarely inland. This photo shows the distinctive red spot on the lower front bill of the adult bird.

Pages 2, 3. This gently rolling north country shows the scattered trees that typify the treeline—where the boreal forest ends and the Arctic tundra begins.

Page 4. The snow goose nests beyond the treeline, particularly on Ellesmere and Baffin Islands. Once mature, the bird remains a striking white color with black wing tips. It is unforgettable when viewed against a hardwood forest backdrop during the fall migration.

Page 8. Cottongrass heads bounce and flow in an Arctic breeze, the equivalent of the sailor's streamer "telltales" in determining wind direction.

Contents

The Last Wilderness

The Arctic begins where the trees stop. Parts of Russia, Scandinavia and Alaska and more than one-third of Canada are Arctic regions, among the last true wilderness areas left on our planet. This book is about the Arctic and the steps that must be taken to ensure its survival.

Living things found in this northern region must be tough to survive, but the system is often termed fragile because it is inhabited by a relatively small number of species. More than three times the number of land mammals exist in the province of Ontario than are found in the vast Northwest Territories; of the 518 Canadian bird species, only 80 breed in the Arctic; south of the treeline there are 10,000 species of insects, but north of it only 500. These limited numbers make the Arctic ecosystem like a wall built with only a few stones — remove one and the whole wall is weakened.

The Arctic is popularly thought of as "the land of ice and snow." In fact, it's probably more accurate to describe it as a cold desert: Ellesmere Island, for example, the most northerly part of Canada, receives only 2.5 inches of snow and rain a year. What falls stays, though, making snow an almost year-round feature of the Arctic landscape. To the Inuit who inhabit this region, this snow has many forms, and hence many names. There is spread-out snow (*aput*), first snow (*apingaut*), saltlike snow (*polaktok*), soft snow (*mauyak*) and snow mixed with water (*massak*). To animals as well as Inuit the many different types of snow are important. Ground snow, or *api*, forms an insulating blanket under which small animals such as lemmings, voles and shrews survive the harsh winter. In the lowest layer, called *pukak*, these mammals establish networks of tunnels where they move and feed. Here the temperature is much warmer than on the surface, where Arctic winds would freeze such small animals solid. The exposed surface snow (*upsik*) can be wind-frozen as hard as cement, allowing caribou, musk oxen, wolves and polar bears to travel easily.

Against the snow's white backdrop move many similarly colored animals: the polar bear, Arctic fox, snowy owl, gyrfalcon, ermine, Arctic hare, ptarmigan and the Arctic wolf. This camouflage is equally important for prey and predator, disguising the hunter as well as the hunted.

But this system could not exist without the plant life that forms the first link in the food chain. Plants sustain the herbivores, such as mice and caribou, which in turn are eaten by fox, wolves and other carnivores. Were the plants to be destroyed, the wolves, indirectly, would die off too.

In the brief spring, summer and fall, the Arctic landscape is transformed into a breathtaking mixture of richly colored shrubs, flowers and lichens. But like the animals, the plants are fragile. They may have thick skins and grow close to the ground to resist cold, but they are not well suited to withstand the damage caused by fire or vehicles. It can take 50 years or more for the tundra to recover from temporary roads or even a single passage by a bulldozer or tractor.

Plants of course depend on water and nutrients from the soil, plus sunlight — energy from the sun is the ultimate driving force for the Arctic system, as it is for all life on earth. But the sunny, warm season is short in the Arctic, forcing all wildlife there to adapt to the cold.

First, there is the basic shape of Arctic species. Most, like the musk ox and polar bear, are streamlined and short legged, allowing them to stay close to the ground. A giraffelike creature could not survive in the Arctic. Species such as the Arctic fox can get closer still to the ground by curling up wrapped in their tails while sleeping, and ptarmigan sleep below the snow's surface in drifts. Indeed, nearly all Arctic species, from caribou to owls, allow snow to drift in around them while resting, for it both serves as an insulating blanket and minimizes exposure to the heat-draining wind. Many Arctic species also have short, stubby ears, noses and tails — long ones can freeze easily and radiate heat away from the body.

In addition to seeking shelter from the cold in snow drifts and ice caves, Arctic animals carry around their own insulation. The polar bear, for example, has hollow fur hairs that contain air — the ideal insulator. And nearly all Arctic fur bearers have an undercoat of guard hairs that provides an inner layer for warmth.

Arctic sea mammals such as seals, whales and walrus also have their own insulation: thick layers of blubber that help keep them warm and store fat for energy. Arctic geese and ducks, too, develop special fat layers during the cold season, plus fuzzy, short down beneath the larger outside feathers. And unlike more southern birds' exposed talons and feet, the snowy owl's and ptarmigan's legs and toes are covered by feathers.

Arctic temperatures can vary as much as 120 Fahrenheit degrees between winter and summer, so protective layers such as feathers, fur or fat change texture and density with the seasons, allowing some creatures to live year round in the extreme northern climate. Only one Arctic mammal — the ground squirrel — hibernates to survive the harsh winter. During its deep, eight-month-long sleep its body temperature drops from the same as a human's to just a few degrees above freezing, lowering its heart rate from 300 beats a minute to three.

Many species migrate south during the winter months. The majority of Arctic bird species, for example, only nest in the north for a few weeks, then move south to regions with warmer climates and more abundant food supplies. One bird that moves against this pattern is the delicate-looking Ross's gull. Only in 1980 was this bird found to nest on mainland Canada, near Churchill, from where it migrates to the High Arctic Islands and Siberia for the winter.

There's a seasonal tide of life moving into and out of the Arctic oceans as well. The Arctic whales — narwhals, belugas and bowheads — need open water to come to the surface to breathe. Therefore in winter, when the inland seas are frozen, these animals move out to the more open ocean. In the eastern Arctic, belugas and narwhals move out to Baffin Bay and Davis Strait in winter, then migrate back in toward the coast and river estuaries after the spring ice breakup.

Just as there are many kinds of snow, there are also many kinds of ice. Being able to "read" ice in the Arctic is essential for survival. Permanent sea ice covers so large an area around the North Pole that this ice lowers the temperature of most of the northern half of

the earth. Pack ice is ice formed at sea, becoming three to six feet thick in the first year and an average of ten feet after five years. Land-fast ice forms along shorelines in the fall and extends further out to sea as winter progresses, then recedes in spring and summer. Both sea ice and land-fast ice can break into ice floes. Pressure ridges as high as six-story buildings are formed when ice floes collide, causing the frozen sheets to buckle, heaving up spectacular broken chunks and walls of ice. Icebergs are large pieces of floating ice that have broken off from fresh-water glaciers on land.

Particularly important to such wildlife as whales and seals are areas of open water in otherwise ice-filled sea. Leads, long lines of open water, allow whales to travel between pack ice and fast ice. Polynias are smaller, roundish areas of open water probably created by strong currents. Some polynias stay open all winter and occur in the same area every year, thus providing ocean oases for wildlife. Polar bears spend most of their time roaming over ice, looking for seals. Arctic foxes also explore ice areas, feeding on the remains of seals left by bears.

The Arctic environment is not a lifeless land of continuous ice and snow, but a source of life. The Arctic is like a sleeping giant, a region of the world that takes in a slow, deep breath during the spring, drawing wildlife up from the south and in from the open seas. There follows a summer of rebirth and growth. Then, slowly, the Arctic giant breaths out in the fall, pouring new life back into the south and the oceans for winter. Left behind are the few fascinating creatures that have adapted to the cold. This cycle repeats itself, one breath per year, over millenia.

Far from being monotonously similar, the Arctic landscape ranges from colorful summer tundra meadows in the south to ice-locked islands in the north. A large part of this land area is composed of rocky, barren flats, but there are also oases of plant life on coastal lowlands and in valleys that serve as concentration areas for such Arctic wildlife as musk oxen, caribou, wolves and waterfowl. Nor is the Arctic ocean environment all flat ice or water; rather, it is made up of ice ridges, cracks, sheets, floes and scattered open water that create essential habitats for Arctic wildlife. In order to survive in the Arctic environment, humans, too, have learned to adapt to this harsh but varied land.

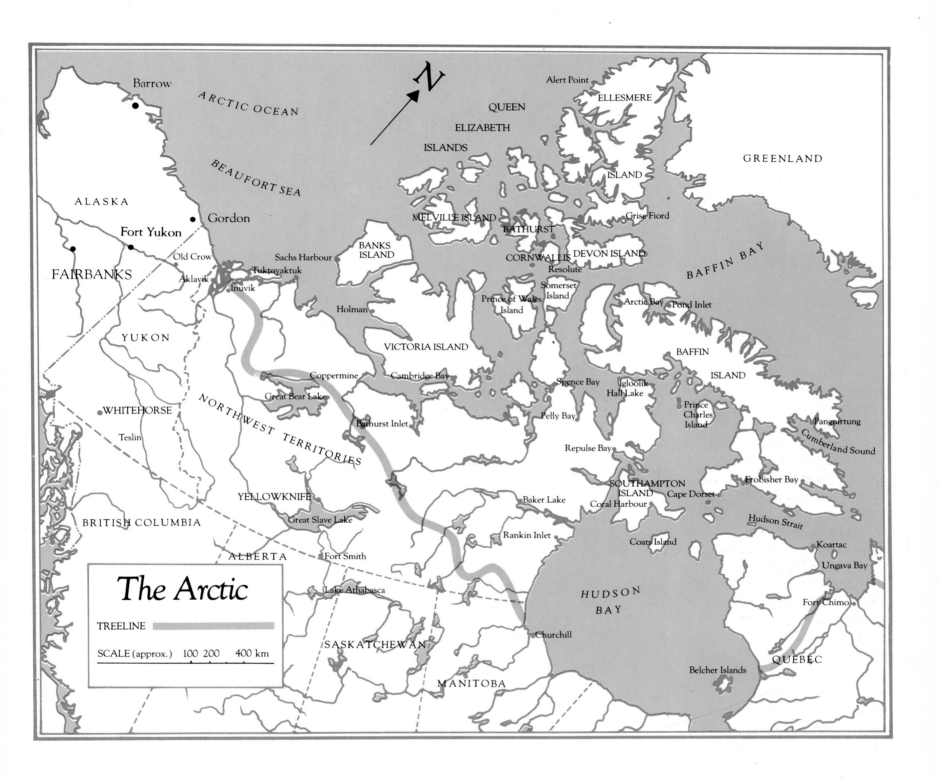

The Arctic

TREELINE

SCALE (approx.)   100 200   400 km

Barrow

ARCTIC OCEAN

BEAUFORT SEA

ALASKA

Gordon

Fort Yukon

Old Crow

Sachs Harbour

Tuktoyaktuk

Aklavik

Inuvik

FAIRBANKS

Holman

YUKON

Coppermine

Cambridge Bay

Great Bear Lake

Bathurst Inlet

VICTORIA ISLAND

WHITEHORSE

NORTHWEST TERRITORIES

Teslin

YELLOWKNIFE

Great Slave Lake

BRITISH COLUMBIA

ALBERTA

Fort Smith

Lake Athabasca

SASKATCHEWAN

MANITOBA

Churchill

Baker Lake

Rankin Inlet

QUEEN ELIZABETH ISLANDS

Alert Point

ELLESMERE

ISLAND

GREENLAND

MELVILLE ISLAND

BATHURST

Grise Fiord

CORNWALLIS

DEVON ISLAND

BAFFIN BAY

BANKS ISLAND

Resolute

Somerset Island

Prince of Wales Island

Arctic Bay

Pond Inlet

BAFFIN

ISLAND

Spence Bay

Igloolik

Hall Lake

Pelly Bay

Prince Charles Island

Pangnirtung

Cumberland Sound

Repulse Bay

Frobisher Bay

SOUTHAMPTON ISLAND

Cape Dorset

Coral Harbour

Hudson Strait

Coats Island

Koartac

Ungava Bay

HUDSON BAY

Fort Chimo

Belcher Islands

QUEBEC

Left. Arctic poppy, one of the most common wildflowers north of the treeline.

Above. Bearberry leaves in autumn. Plants like these make the tundra come alive with color.

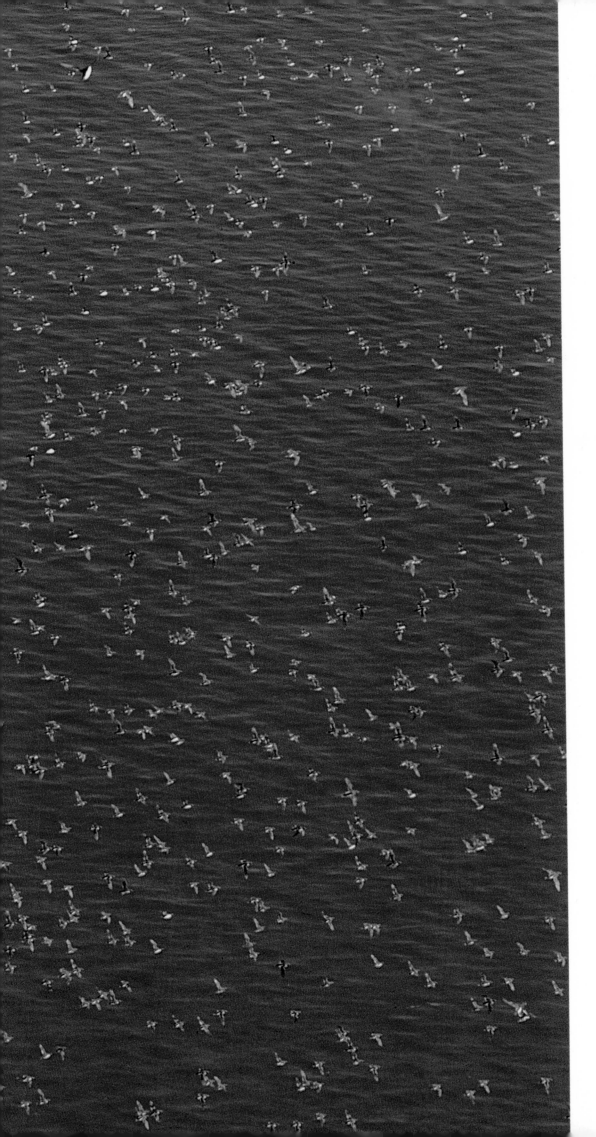

Birds of the Arctic

Thick-billed murres fill an Arctic sky. These colonial nesters are typically concentrated in large numbers during the breeding season.

A rare and exciting sight, eggs in a wild nest of the endangered peregrine falcon.

The only distinctly fork-tailed Canadian gull is
the Sabine's gull, which nests in low wet tundra,
lakes and coastal areas. This bird migrates south
along the Pacific coast to British Columbia.

A freshly-hatched herring gull waits for its brother or sister to appear. This is the same gull seen in the south and commonly called a "seagull". It is broadly distributed throughout Canada and in the southern Arctic.

Unlike the herring gull, which it resembles, this
Thayer's gull will nest in the high Arctic Islands,
usually on coastal cliffs. It winters as far south as
California.

Left. The white wing patches and red feet of the black guillemot are shown nicely here. This fish-eating bird breeds along the coasts of the eastern Arctic and also winters in the Arctic near openings in the pack ice.

Above. The Iceland gull breeds in Canada on the southeastern coast of Baffin Island, and migrates as far south as Virginia, with a few stopping off on the Great Lakes. The Iceland population flies south to the British Isles.

Overleaf. All sandpipers may look the same but there are important differences. Here, a pair of pectoral sandpipers are feeding in shallow water. The male inflates his throat in courtship, making him look unlike any other shorebird.

Left, above. A Baird's sandpiper nests on the tundra in the high Arctic. This bird "fuels up" and develops extra energy for its extraordinary migration all the way to South America.

Left, below. The light-colored breast and underparts account for the name of the buff-breasted sandpiper. This one is nesting in the remote islands of the western Arctic. It will winter in Argentina.

Above. The stilt sandpiper earns its name from the long legs and bill which distinguish it from others. Although we know this relatively large shorebird nests in remote areas of the Arctic, much of its breeding range remains a mystery.

Above. Golden eagles, which have a wingspan of over seven feet, can still be found in the more mountainous western Arctic. Their nest is usually on a cliff, made of sticks and lined with softer material. Their favorite food is ground squirrels.

Right. The common murre breeds along the coast of Labrador and Newfoundland, and in the North Pacific as far as Alaska. Here they are in a typical colony.

This female northern phalarope is larger and brighter than the male during breeding season. Phalaropes are shore birds that swim for long periods in spinning motions, perhaps to stir up food.

The red phalarope has a rich chestnut-red coloring entirely underneath which distinguishes it from the others. The feet have small membranes to help with swimming, which these birds do more than other shore birds.

These young red phalaropes will grow quickly in the Arctic, storing energy, and then will migrate south down either the Atlantic or Pacific coast for winter.

The northern fulmar is normally found fishing
over the open ocean, but at nesting time it lays
one egg on a bare rock ledge along steep cliffs.
A Baffin island fulmar colony had 200,000 birds.

Left, above. Tree sparrows breed above the treeline, but on the mainland. They mark the arrival of fall when they arrive in southern Canada.

Left, below. A tree sparrow nest photographed at Inuvik in the Northwest Territories. The white lining is probably made from cottongrass heads.

Above. Four or five speckled eggs will fill this nest of the white-crowned sparrow, which makes itself at home in dwarf birch and willow on the tundra.

Overleaf. A gyrfalcon nest, or eyrie, overlooking Arctic waters. Controversy exists about whether first-year or "passage" birds should be captured for export to Middle East falconers.

Above. The Arctic sun reveals the rich color of this golden plover, which is supervising a day-old chick.

Right, above. A black-bellied plover hunts the tide line for food.

Right, below. The semipalmated plover has partly webbed toes to help it move around in shallow water while feeding. The nest is often near the sea, on beaches or gravel bars, and lined with seaweed or bits of shell.

Above. A typical thick-billed murre colony. There is no nest. Eggs are simply laid and hatched on the bare rock.

Right. This is the Atlantic variant of the common murre, which has a distinct white eye-ring and a white line back of the eye. Usually only one pear-shaped egg is laid on the bare rock, but this bird appears to have two.

Here is a savannah sparrow nesting at Churchill.
This bird is found throughout mainland Canada,
but does not nest in the Arctic Islands. It benefits
man by feeding on weed seeds and insects.

A long-tailed jaeger gobbles up a random Arctic morsel—probably a young bird. The long-tailed is the smallest of the jaegers, though its tail makes it appear larger.

Left, above. Recognized by everyone, in its many races and subspecies, the Canada goose is most likely headed for the Arctic when it is spotted in the familiar spring V-formation. Pairs mate for life.

Left, below. Three Canada goose goslings explore a sub-Arctic environment near Churchill, Manitoba.

Above. The white-fronted goose is found throughout the world's Arctic, but only west of Hudson Bay in North America. North American birds winter in British Columbia and Mexico. Birds from Greenland, Iceland and Scandinavia winter in North Africa, India and even China.

Left. Thick-billed murres breed along the entire eastern Arctic coast. They have been used as a food species by the Inuit.

Above. A female ptarmigan protects her brood, probably seven to ten chicks. Ptarmigan are hunted heavily by many predators; fortunately they have large families.

A hoary redpoll incubates eggs in a nest near the Anderson River in the Northwest Territories. Redpolls may return to the same nest in successive breeding seasons, and they often stay in the Arctic for the winter.

This common redpoll has taken up residence in a
low spruce tree. Notice the cosy, warm lining of
feathers and cottongrasses to ensure that the
incubating eggs withstand spring cold spells.

Above. One of the most beautiful and subtly colored shorebirds, the whimbrel reaches a length of 1.5 feet. The downward curving bill helps watchers identify the bird, as do the distinctive headstripes.

Right, above. The water pipit feeds on the ground, walking rather than hopping, and wagging its longish tail. This is a classic ground nest. Underneath the bird are four or five well-camouflaged eggs.

Right, below. A whimbrel nest on the tundra is an important find because the bird's breeding area is still not well understood.

Left. A delicate semipalmated sandpiper nestles down among Arctic wildflowers. Both male and female incubate the eggs for an 18-day period before hatching.

Above. The small Ross's goose nests in only two or three very localized Arctic areas, then migrates to the Sacramento and San Joaquin valleys in California. Note the pink bill and reddish feet.

Left, above. A parasitic jaeger preens itself on the tundra. Jaegers are opportunistic pirates which feed on almost anything alive or dead.

Left, below. A snowy owl nest, as usual, out in the open on the rolling tundra, where the female will incubate the eggs for more than a month in the face of Arctic winds.

Above. The snowy owl often appears as an indistinguishable white hump of feathers on the tundra. Notice that even the bill is protected from cold by facial feathers. Lemmings taken by day are its main prey.

The whistling swan is now officially called the tundra swan because it nests in the Arctic. Its voice is somewhat like that of the Canada goose, but more musical.

A whistling, or tundra, swan, with two young
cygnets, leads them to water on an Arctic
landscape.

The only white falcon, and the largest in the world, the gyrfalcon feeds its young on a cliff slope. Gyrfalcons usually feed on ptarmigan, but this nest appears to hold the remains of an Arctic hare.

The dunlin nests on the ground, often near a salt marsh, where it can feed on tiny crustaceans left behind by the tide.

Overleaf. The blue goose is really a phase of the snow goose, but its markings are distinct enough to have earned it a separate name. The two phases commonly mix together and both raise young on the tundra.

The cheerful, small snow bunting is usually seen flying low, in large undulating flocks, over a snowscape. For southern Canadians, it is a harbinger of winter; for those in the Arctic, it foretells spring.

A typical snow bunting nest in a rock crevice, lined with grass or feathers. These eggs need to be incubated for only 13 days before hatching.

Previous page. A rough-legged hawk looks out from its Arctic nest site. This is the only hawk in Canada that breeds exclusively in the Arctic. For protection against the cold it has legs completely feathered down to the toes.

Above. The small white-rumped sandpiper is only seven or eight inches long. The female incubates the eggs in a nest on a mound in wet Arctic tundra areas. Urban North Americans only see this bird when it is migrating in spring and fall.

Right. The common raven is an important scavenger throughout northern Canada and Alaska, feeding on carrion such as old wolf-kills. It is much larger than a crow, with a heavier bill and noticeable throat feathers.

The Hudsonian godwit is a large shorebird whose range in North America is still not fully understood. This one was nesting near Churchill in 1971. We do know that it summers in special locations of the sub-Arctic and winters in South America.

A squadron of long-tailed jaegers scans the Arctic
landscape for food. This fierce predator kills
young birds of all kinds.

The Lapland longspur likes open spaces. It lives,
nests and feeds on the ground. The male,
pictured here by his nest, has a magnificent call
which floats over the Arctic landscape in
summer.

One snow goose gosling has hatched, one is
breaking out, and the other two can't be far
behind. Note the abundance of goose down in
the nest to ensure warmth during incubation.

Five young ravens are being raised in this rock-ledge nest. These hearty birds are able to make a living in the Arctic year-round.

Newly-hatched wild peregrine falcon chicks are a
rare but encouraging sight for conservationists,
because the Arctic peregrine has been officially
classified as a threatened species in Canada.

Left. A male willow ptarmigan seems to be alert and somewhat alarmed, as he peers from his position on a tundra tussock. Note the insulating feathers all the way down the legs and toes.

Above. The breeding range of the oldsquaw duck corresponds almost perfectly with the area north of the treeline. The female will hatch six to eight young.

A winter willow ptarmigan's plumage will cause it
to literally disappear against a snowy backdrop.
The similar rock ptarmigan has a black streak
through the eye.

The russet back of a ruddy turnstone glows in the
light of its Arctic nesting spot. These birds like
pebbly beaches and coastlines with tidal debris
when they probe for food.

Above. The horned lark is the only native lark in Canada. It is a famous early arrival everywhere, in fields and open land. The twinkling bell-like spring song is often heard from on high, even though the bird is out of sight.

Right, above. Young red-breasted merganser downies already show the distinctive "sawbill" of this fish-eating duck. The bill has special backward-pointing "teeth" to help hold its slippery prey.

Right, below. Two adult black brant geese lead six downy goslings past tundra flowers to water. This bird nests in the high Arctic and can be distinguished from the Canada goose by its black breast and lack of white cheeks.

The black-legged kittiwake is strictly an ocean
bird, coming ashore on North Baffin Island and
Newfoundland only for the breeding season.

The whitewashed rocks and nesting birds indicate
a colony of black-legged kittiwakes. This ocean
bird prefers to build a well-cupped nest of
seaweed or grass.

Left. A rock ptarmigan shows adult summer plumage which helps it blend perfectly with a partially snowcovered tundra.

Above. The Arctic tern nests throughout the Arctic. Terns dive for their food and fly with their beaks angled downward. Gulls, on the other hand, usually land, then eat, and they fly with bills extended straight out.

Left above. A male king eider in full breeding plumage shows the unmistakable markings of this truly Arctic duck. His voice in courtship is a musical low cooing sound.

Left below. An eider duck nest, probably that of the king eider, judging from the darker down than that used by the common eider. Common eiders also tend to nest in colonies but kings are more solitary.

Above. Just a bit of the distinctive marking shows on this nesting red-throated loon which is tidying up its nest.

Above. The Arctic loon is the smallest loon in Canada, though it breeds in all the other Arctic countries as well. Unlike ducks and geese, loons have very pointed bills. They are excellent divers.

Right, above. The yellow-billed loon is often confused with the common loon, which has a dark bill. Also, their breeding ranges do not appear to overlap, the yellow-billed being found in the central Arctic, the common all across temperate Canada.

Right, below. The female common eider duck incubates her eggs for twenty-eight to twenty-nine days. A down lining is added to the nest as the eggs are laid.

Life in a Hard Land

The Arctic is the land of the Inuit, which means "the people." Although the first ancestors of Indian groups now found further south probably came to North America from Asia 25,000 to 30,000 years ago, the forefathers of modern Inuit are believed to have come from Asia through Alaska sometime in the last 3,000 to 5,000 years. Later, they spread across the Arctic as far east as Greenland; there is evidence Inuit settlements were established on Ellesmere Island long before the days of the Roman Empire. By the time of the first European contact in 1600, the Inuit are believed to have numbered about 6,000 in North America, although experts disagree about this estimate.

What *is* certain is that the Inuit have traditionally been absolutely dependent on Arctic wildlife for food, clothing, fuel and shelter. The early Inuit were primarily a coastal people, living in small, temporary villages along the Arctic coast where they caught fish and hunted seals, walrus, beluga, narwhal, bowhead whale and polar bears. They also collected the eggs of and hunted the ocean birds, ducks and geese found along the coast. The degree to which the early Inuit relied on caribou is not clearly understood. It may be that with the arrival of commercial whalers between 1650 and 1850 (from Europe in the eastern Arctic and from America in the west) caribou became more important as whales became scarcer. This theory is bolstered by evidence that during this period village life gave way to more seasonal hunting camps, suggesting the transition to an inland, caribou-oriented culture.

In any case, the traditional Inuit developed an immense knowledge of wildlife and many clever ways of capturing prey. Fish were taken with three-pronged spears (*kakivats*) or corraled in rock wiers. Seals were harpooned through holes in the ice, with delicate floats giving advance warning of a seal coming up for air, or speared as they lay on the ice basking in the sun. Walrus and whales were pursued in large, open boats called *umiaks*. Because of the danger posed by whales' size, the Inuit devised harpoons with removable

heads to whose lines were attached floats fashioned from seal bladders or other inflatable objects. Once tired by the effort of battling the floats, the whales could easily be found and killed. Caribou were herded past strategically placed stone figures, called *inukshuks*, built to look like men, some of which still dot the Arctic landscape. Caribou were driven into corals and finished off with arrows; or chased into lakes or rivers where they were harpooned from kayaks. Birds were captured using bolas — stones tied to leather thongs — which would wrap around the bird's legs and wings if the weapon was thrown accurately. Polar bears were first tired by being chased by dogs, then speared.

This wildlife provided the Inuit with more than food. Clothing was made of a multitude of furs, hides, skins, even feathers. Boots (*kamiks*) were constructed from sealskin and sometimes covered by an extra overshoe turned fur side out (*mungwa*), trousers from caribou hide or polar bear skin, and light shirts from animal hides or bird skins turned feather side in. The Inuit outer garments were parkas with the fur side of the hide turned against the wearer's skin; to further guard against cold, a second parka with the fur side out was sometimes worn. Mitts of waterproof sealskin were used when handling wet harpoon or fishing lines.

The Inuit fashioned whalebone, teeth and ivory into harpoons, arrowheads, small carvings, fish hooks, needles, tent and boat frames, tools, cooking utensils and much more. Hides and sinews were used for lines, boat skins, tents and roofs on stone houses. Animal fats became fuel in stone lamps (*kudliks*) that served for cooking, heating and light.

Although local wildlife populations were no doubt reduced, there is no evidence that traditional Inuit hunting actually exterminated any Arctic species. To the Inuit, wildlife represented both physical and spiritual survival, and so had to be treated with respect. Hunters believed that all creatures had spirits that, if abused, could tell fellow animals not to allow themselves to be caught.

Hunting was a partially religious act involving charms and ceremonies to ensure future success.

With European contact, things changed. Just as the fur trade further south introduced Indians to the notion that skins and hides could be bartered for items such as firearms, cooking pots, axes, fishnets, and other goods, so the whalers had a similar impact on the Inuit. But these Europeans also introduced something far more sinister and deadly: such white man's diseases as tuberculosis and smallpox. Entire populations were struck, and in many cases decimated, the Inuit of the Mackenzie Delta in the western Arctic being virtually wiped out.

The coming of the Europeans affected the Inuit in other ways. Species on which they depended suffered greatly as a result of commercial demand. The bowhead whale was brought to the brink of extinction; musk oxen were killed in large numbers to provide meat for whalers. Another legacy — such modern hunting equipment as rifles, nets, motorboats, snowmobiles — hastened the depletion of already reduced stocks. In recent years, the building of roads and establishment of mines and oil exploration camps, particularly in the western Arctic, has led to further pressure on species such as caribou by nonnative hunters.

Today there are perhaps 20,000 Inuit in Canada and Alaska. Southern food is very expensive in the Arctic because it must usually be flown in. Nor is it as nutritious as wild game or "country food." Caribou meat, for example, contains about fifty percent more protein than beef. Wildlife remains an important component of the modern-day Inuit diet. Arctic char, whitefish, lake trout and ciscoes are staples in many communities. Beluga whales continue to be hunted in both the eastern and western Arctic and Hudson Bay, primarily for the *muktuk* (skin and a thin layer of blubber). Narwhal *muktuk* is prized in the eastern Arctic communities such as Arc-

tic Bay and Pond Inlet. Ringed seals are still basic to the Inuit economy throughout the Arctic, supplying food, skin that is made into clothing and handicrafts and the seal pelts that are sold commercially — an important source of cash income.

Ducks and geese and their eggs are also important sources of food throughout the Arctic. In 1983 a World Wildlife Fund team studying whales along the north shore of Baffin Island discovered, by accident, what they believed to be the first known breeding colony of dovekies in Canada. Dovekies, small sea birds, were previously thought to nest only in Greenland, and the researchers were thrilled. But the amused local Inuit set them straight: "If you wanted to know where they were, all you had to do was ask. We've been catching them for generations."

There is some controversy surrounding modern Inuit use of wildlife. Should narwhals and walrus be taken if only their tusks are sought for ivory? Should the Alaskan Inuit be hunting bowhead whales if these animals are truly endangered? Should gyrfalcons be captured for export to the Middle East sport falconry market? How many polar bears can be killed every year before the population becomes endangered?

The Inuit may have been the first humans to depend on Arctic wildlife, but they are no longer the only ones. Photographers, naturalists, scientists and artists from around the world are taking an active interest in the north. Churchill, once famous for its grain elevators, now is better known as the polar bear capital of the world.

Tourism may well become the number one industry for the Arctic, attracting wildlife enthusiasts who can contribute needed cash to a people no longer able to depend simply on the land for survival. Just as wildlife has been crucial to the lives of the Arctic people in the past, it will continue to sustain them, in a different way, in the future.

Mammals
of the
Arctic

Left. These are juvenile Arctic hares foraging on
the tundra. Two are alert with ears upright.
If alarmed, they will bound off—hopping,
kangaroo-style, on their hind feet only.

Left. A mature Arctic hare can weigh seven to twelve pounds. The large feet are padded with bristly hairs for protection. This one is in a meadow of cottongrass.

Above. An immature Arctic hare stretches in the low sunlight of Ellesmere Island. Note the long, strong front claws for digging for food in the snow.

Left, above. The Arctic fox is important to the Arctic ecosystem because it controls vole and lemming populations. It is important to man as well, because it is the main species taken by Arctic trappers.

Left, below. A male red fox greets a female who has returned with a fresh kill.

Above. This red fox scoots across the tunara holding an Arctic ground squirrel.

Overleaf. There are at least nine races of the red fox in Canada, including two in the Arctic.

A red fox kit relaxes near a typical denning site—open country with water not far away. Red foxes aren't often found in densely forested areas.

An Arctic fox showing signs of its lighter winter coat. These animals live on lemmings and voles everywhere. Coastal foxes have been called "marine mammals" because they hunt the ice for seals killed by polar bears.

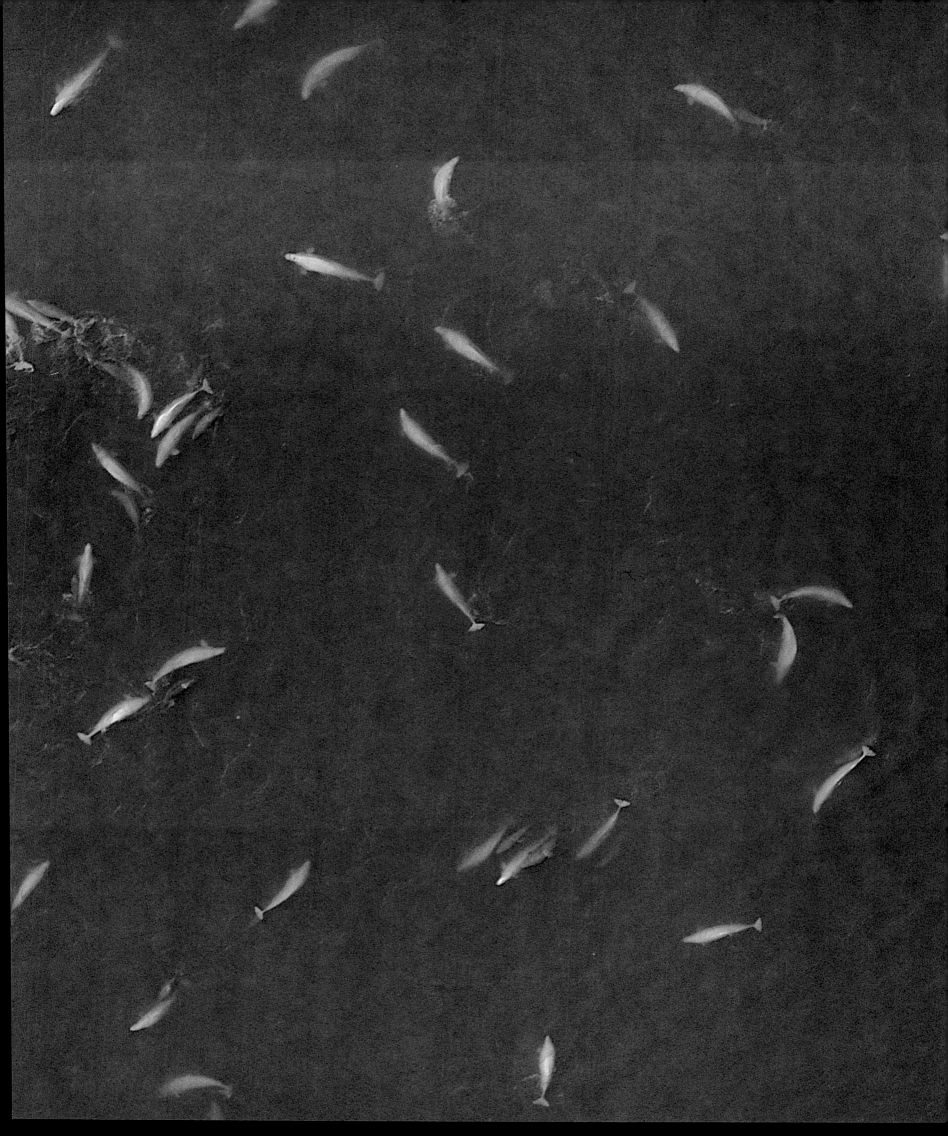

Previous page. Beluga whales are seen from an aircraft straight overhead. Some of the smaller slate-colored calves can be seen with the larger white females.

Above. The bowhead whale is an endangered species, brought to the brink of extinction by commercial whaling. This is the largest Arctic mammal, reaching a length of sixty-five feet.

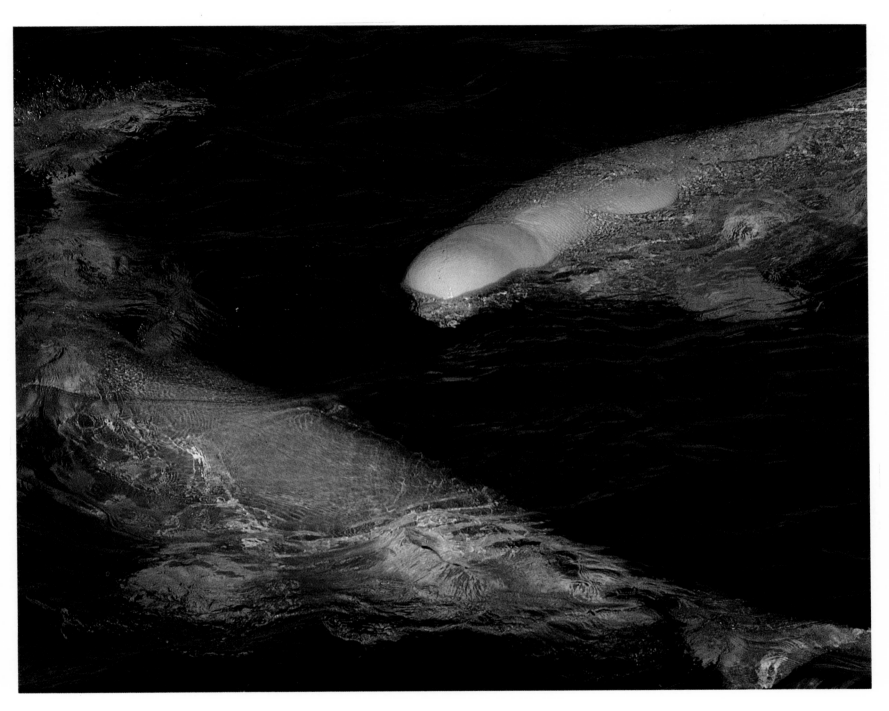

Two beluga whales near the surface. Although these whales are still generally abundant in the Arctic, some local populations are severely threatened.

Left, above. Beluga, or white, whales gather in a summer river estuary. Scientists now believe belugas come here to shed their old skins by rubbing on rocks and gravel.

Left, below. Narwhals number somewhere between ten and thirty thousand in Canada, but we need to have a more accurate count because they are important as food for the Inuit of the eastern Arctic.

Above. The ringed seal is the smallest seal in Canada, only 4.5 feet long, but a most important species in the Arctic because of its very broad distribution. It is the main prey species for polar bears.

A female harp seal with her whitecoat pup, born on the open ice off Canada's east coast. Though this seal is not endangered, the commercial hunting of the young seals has been the source of world controversy.

The harbor seal is the best-known seal in Canada. They tend to group together up on land but hunt alone for fish and molluscs. Harbor seals, unlike ringed seals, are not found in the central Arctic.

Above. The harp seal gets its name from a roughly horseshoe-shaped dark pattern on the back and shoulders of the adult male. Adult harp seals have traditionally been taken by the Inuit in the eastern Arctic.

Right. The sensitive bristly moustache of the walrus is used to feel for molluscs on the ocean bottom and the tusks aid in digging them up.

A hooded seal displays the inflatable nasal sac
which is characteristic of the male of this species.

Much less is known about this hooded seal than about the harp seal, which has attracted so much public attention, even though both are taken in the spring hunt. Hooded seals are almost twice as large. They frequent the eastern Arctic only.

Left. Walruses commonly "haul out" on land in large numbers after feeding. Here they bask in the sun, perhaps for as long as a week without feeding if the weather is nice.

Above. These walruses appear alarmed and are diving. Apart from man, only polar bears and killer whales prey on walruses and then probably only on the young ones. A big bull can weigh 1.5 tons.

Page 110. The Arctic ground squirrel is the only Arctic mammal that truly hibernates for the winter. The dens are about 2 feet below the surface and lined with grasses, leaves and even animal hair.

Page 111. The Arctic or Parry's ground squirrel is the largest ground squirrel in North America, and an extremely important prey species for Arctic wildlife such as foxes and golden eagles. This squirrel's burrow is surrounded by fireweed.

Above. The ermine is a fascinating and fierce tiny carnivore that eats voles and lemmings primarily, but it will tackle hares too. It efficiently kills its prey by biting through the spine at the base of the skull. Ermine store small dead animals for winter food.

Right. The wolverine, the largest member of the weasel family, is legendary in the north for its ferocity and cunning. It is also officially classified as "rare". Many people live a lifetime in the Arctic and never see one.

Left. An Arctic vole peeks up from its tundra habitat. Voles are important food species for Arctic birds of prey, foxes and weasels.

Above. The collared lemming turns white in the winter, when it lives in runways under the snow. In summer, lemmings live in shallow burrows four to eight inches below the tundra, with separate chambers for resting, raising young and toilet areas.

Previous page. Barren-ground caribou ford an Arctic river. Despite their large hooves, which help them swim, many young calves are lost in particularly dangerous river crossings.

Above. Peary caribou travel in small groups rather than in large herds like their barren-ground cousins. This is officially classified as a threatened species in Canada. It is the smallest, lightest colored and most northerly caribou.

Signs of life on the land. These are caribou trails
used for centuries by hundreds of thousands of
animals.

Every caribou cow knows her calf, probably as
much by smell as by sight. A caribou calf is
born ready to move with the herd. It can outrun a
man when it is only a day old.

Barren-ground caribou spread out and feeding on the tundra. This is a relaxed scene when compared to the compulsive movement of migration in spring and fall.

Caribou antlers appear in March, grow until summer, harden by mid-September when velvet is scraped off (this photo), become polished and clean by October and are shed from November to February.

Barren-ground caribou on the move. Declines in some herds have led to the establishment of cooperative management boards which include a majority of Inuit members.

Overleaf. Heeding a call that has become genetically encoded through successive generations, this herd of barren-ground caribou restlessly moves south to the wintering grounds.

Left. Two healthy caribou work their way up a trail in mid-summer. Both males and females can develop antlers, but the male's are larger.

Above. The "ghost of the tundra", a threatened Peary caribou wanders in a never-ending search for food in the harsh environment of the high Arctic islands.

Overleaf. Barren-ground caribou dot the north slope in the Yukon. This critical caribou range has been proposed for a national park.

Left. This musk ox calf has its juvenile winter coat, an intermediate stage between the short, curly, newborn coat and the adult hair which will develop in the third winter.

Above. The profile of a musk ox, a classic Arctic animal: short, compact, stocky body, stubby tail, long, thick hair over the entire body, short limbs, well protected ears, and specially adapted hooves for ice and snow.

Left. This massive coat protects the musk ox, but it was almost its undoing. Between 1864–1916 over 15,000 hides were shipped from Canada for sleigh rugs. By 1930, only 500 musk oxen remained on the mainland, but now they are increasing.

Above. The well-known defense posture of musk oxen crowding together and facing out. When alarmed, the herd will also run closely packed together.

Grizzly bears do frequent the barren-lands; in fact, the word "Arctic" is included in the Latin name for this bear, *Ursus arctos*. Along with the polar bear, this animal deserves respect and caution. Grizzlies have poor eyesight but excellent hearing and sense of smell.

A grizzly winter den. Hibernation is short for these bears, which may still be found on the tundra in December, and are often seen digging their way out of the snow in March.

An Arctic grizzly bear emerges from the water.
These bears have a very slow rate of reproduction
because the females can only breed every other
year and they are not sexually mature until six or
seven.

A grizzly finishes off its favorite food, a fish. In fact, grizzlies eat almost anything, including caribou meat cached for later use by man.

Although threatened in other parts of the world, most North American polar bear populations are still relatively healthy. The western Hudson Bay population is the most productive in the world.

Polar bears have often been observed playing on thin ice, falling through, swimming under, and butting their heads up.

Canada has one of the last healthy wolf
populations in the world, with many subspecies
in all parts of the country. The Arctic wolf still
roams much as it always has, and symbolizes the
wilderness quality of the north for many people.

Whenever the wolf has competed with man, the wolf has been the loser. In the Arctic, too, there are proposals to control wolf numbers because they compete with man for caribou meat.

Above. The Arctic wolf is unique not only for its light color but for the stiff hair that grows between its foot pads to protect them against cold. Wolves prey on many Arctic species, but caribou is the most important.

Right. Although it needs some treed cover for the winter, the moose does range into Arctic regions, especially during the summer season. Its hair can reach a six-inch length on the shoulders and neck for Arctic protection.

In the course of underwater browsing, moose look up regularly to breathe and to see if there's anything to be concerned about. They have excellent hearing and sense of smell.

Above. A big bull moose, shedding velvet from his antlers, browses against an autumn Arctic backdrop of scattered trees and tundra.

Overleaf. Moose are browsers on shrubs and twigs, rather than grazers on grass or lichens like caribou. The moose's favorite summer food is the leaves and stems of water lilies.

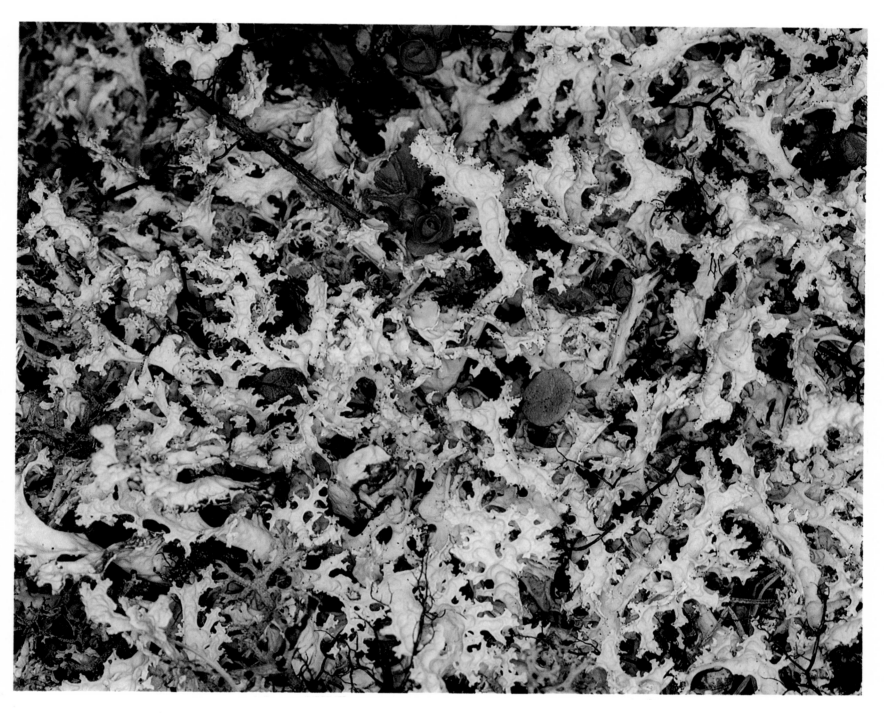

Left. Scattered spruce, lichens and mosses mark the northern treeline. These remnant caribou antlers have been bleached white by exposure to sun and Arctic wind. The boulder is testimony to rubble left behind by receding glaciers from the last Ice Age.

Above. This is the kind of lichen growth sought after by caribou digging out feeding craters in snow during the long Arctic winter.

Above. Lichens growing on rocks are part of everyone's memory of the Arctic. The larger lichens are scraped free by caribou for food, particularly in winter when other plants are dormant and unavailable to them.

Right. A dwarf willow flowers on Baffin Island. The form and general appearance of this plant remind us that the Arctic is a cold desert.

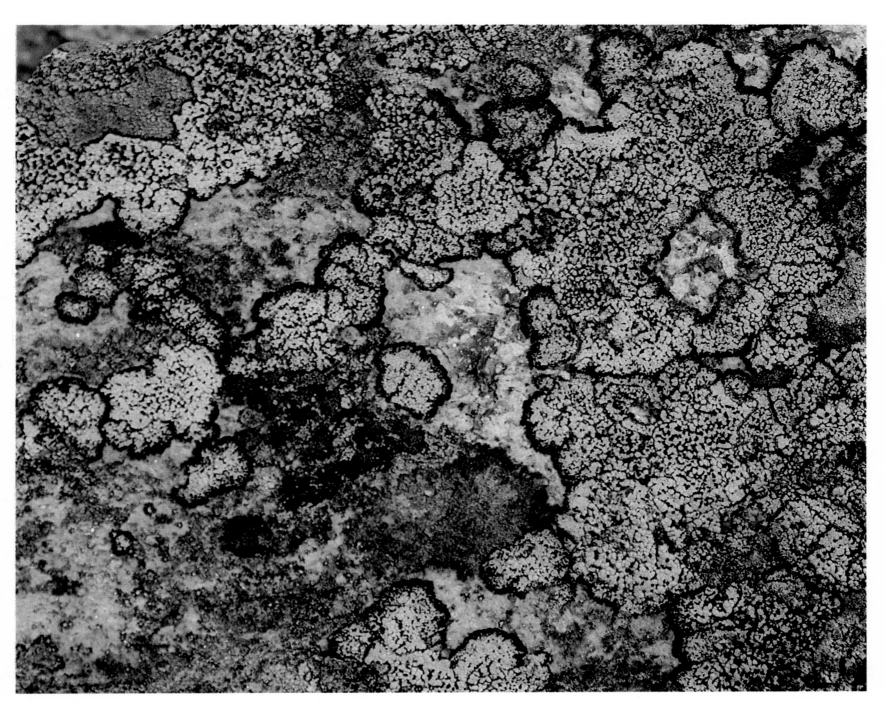

Left. A beautiful spring woolly lousewort blooms on Ellesmere Island. This is a member of the snapdragon family, which is found throughout Canada. Farmers in the south thought cattle which ate this plant got lice, hence the name.

Above. These Arctic lichens are flowerless plants composed of fungi and algae which aid each other and grow together.

Conserving the Legacy

At present we are losing species from the earth at the rate of one a day and many other forms of wildlife are endangered, brought to the brink of extinction by man. By endangering the components of a system we jeopardize the system itself, and the Arctic is no exception.

So far, two Arctic species — the bowhead whale and Eskimo curlew — have been officially declared endangered by the Committee on the Status of Endangered Wildlife in Canada. Two others — the peregrine falcon and Peary caribou — are considered threatened; and three more — the wolverine, the ivory gull and Ross's gull — are listed as rare. All must therefore be considered at risk and are deserving of special concern.

The bowhead whale is best described as a tractor trailer-sized tadpole, with a huge mouth of sieves called baleen plates through which it screens tiny ocean crustaceans. It can reach a length of sixty-five feet and weigh more than seventy-five tons, making it the largest of the true Arctic whales.

There are two distinct populations of bowheads in the Arctic, one in the east, which has dropped from about 7,000 members to a few hundred, the other in the west, which now numbers roughly 3,000 to 5,000, down from an estimated 15,000. These drastic reductions are a direct result of commercial whaling carried out in the seventeenth to twentieth centuries.

The International Whaling Commission no longer permits any commercial killing of bowhead whales, although the Inuit of Alaska's north coast continue to take a few every year. Canadian regulations adopted in 1979 prohibit the hunting and killing of this species by anyone, except by special permission and license issued by the minister of Fisheries and Oceans; to date, no permits have been issued. However, despite this protection, there is great concern about the bowhead's future, for these whales are slow to reproduce, with females bearing a single calf only every few years.

In the nineteenth century there were mil-lions of Eskimo curlews, long-billed subtly marked shorebirds about the size of a pigeon. Today there are perhaps twenty left, and many experts believe these birds are already extinct since none has been photographed since 1962.

As in the case of the bowhead, the blame for this destruction of a species lies primarily with man. Commercial hunting between 1890 and 1895 severely reduced Eskimo curlew populations, although the bird weighs scarcely a pound. Fishermen and homesteaders also killed them in large numbers for food, especially after the extinction of the passenger pigeon. Their numbers were further depleted as the grasslands that had traditionally provided food along their migration route became cultivated as settlement spread. Ocean storms may also have killed large numbers as the curlews migrated to South America over the Atlantic Ocean.

The Eskimo curlew — if it still exists — is protected in the U.S. and Canada by the Migratory Birds Convention, and both countries have officially listed it as an endangered species, which means harsh penalties for anyone caught disturbing it.

The peregrine falcon found in the Canadian Arctic is of the *tundrius* subspecies, one of three recognized subspecies in Canada. It has come to be threatened largely as a result of pesticide poisoning. Pesticides applied to crops in areas further south where these birds winter are eaten by insects that are consumed by smaller birds, which in turn are the prey of peregrines. As a pesticide moves up the food chain in this way, it becomes more and more concentrated in the bodies of the prey species, and predators at the top of the chain consequently are exposed to high levels of these poisons. While the pesticide may not kill the peregrines directly, it can result in the failure of females to lay fertile eggs.

In recent years restrictions on the use of such pesticides as DDT and DDE in Canada have significantly reduced the impact of these chemicals on peregrines. At the same time, programs involving the breeding of peregrines in captivity for release in wild areas,

155

including the Arctic, have increased their numbers.

Other threats still face this falcon, however. High levels of pesticides continue to exist in the peregrine's South American wintering grounds. Peregrines are also much prized for falconry — they are the swiftest creatures on earth, able to dive at speeds of 155 miles an hour — and so have become targets for poachers, who catch them for sale in the Middle East, where they command high prices.

The Peary caribou is another threatened Arctic species. These unique animals, the smallest caribou in Canada, have long, white hairs in their winter coats that have earned them the name "ghosts of the Arctic." They are found only in Canada's high Arctic islands, particularly the western Queen Elizabeth Islands.

Unlike the barren-ground caribou, Peary caribou do not travel in large herds. Rather, they band together in sparsely scattered groups of three or four in response to a very limited food supply. They wander from island to island and out over sea ice, searching for sedges, grasses, flowers, shrubs and lichens.

The enemy of these animals has been weather, not man. Between 1961 and 1974 the Peary caribou population of the Queen Elizabeth Islands declined by more than ninety percent. In 1977-78 much of the Banks Island population perished after a severe ice storm struck the island in the fall.

While little can be done to shield the Peary caribou from the vagaries of the weather, it is essential that their already limited numbers are not further eroded by human activities. The Territorial Lands Act protects these animals from harassment by aircraft or disturbance by vehicles and ground installations associated with oil and gas exploration or other industrial development. Hunting is also controlled, particularly at times when the caribou's numbers are low due to bad weather or short food supply.

The wolverine, ivory gull, and Ross's gull are all regarded as rare in Canada, which means that these animals naturally occur in low numbers or in very restricted areas. Because they are already vulnerable, rare species can be particularly harmed by human activity.

The wolverine, the largest member of the weasel family in Canada, is about the size of a bear cub. Wolverines are found in small numbers throughout the Arctic, but are probably more abundant on the mainland than on Arctic islands. These animals' strength, stamina, ferocity and cunning are legendary in the north — it is said that a wolverine will defend its food against even a wolf or grizzly. Hated by trappers because it raids traplines and cabins, the wolverine is also prized for its "frost-free" fur.

The demand for its pelt is one reason the wolverine population is decreasing, although it faces other threats: poison set for wolves that also affects wolverines; lack of caribou carcasses for food; and civilization's encroachment on wilderness areas.

The beautiful ivory gull is the only gull with pure white feathers and pure black legs. This far-ranging, nomadic bird is found in other regions in the world, but in Canada is known only to breed on Seymour and Ellesmere islands in the high Arctic. There are probably only 2,000 or so of these birds in Canada.

If ivory gulls are disturbed when nesting they may react by abandoning the colony or even destroying their eggs and young. These birds lived undisturbed for centuries in remote areas, but now, aircraft and snow vehicles permit access to the quiet home of the ivory gull and the result could be disasterous. In Canada, all previously known breeding areas have been abandoned, and the birds have also disappeared from major colonies in Sweden.

Ross's gull was declared a new wildlife species for mainland Canada in 1980, when it was first discovered to nest near Churchill. Its identifying features are a delicate black line, or "necklace," around the throat and a slight rosiness of color down the breast. Ross's gull normally nests in Siberia, but there are also

records from Greenland and the Canadian Cheyne Islands.

The World Wildlife Fund has been observing and protecting the new colony of eight to twelve birds that is trying to establish itself at Churchill. Because of their rarity these birds have brought literally thousands of birdwatchers, naturalists and photographers to Churchill. They even attracted a thief who in 1981 stole one of the nests with its eggs, probably for sale on the international egg collector's market. It has been fascinating to watch the Ross's gulls struggle with harsh weather, foxes, weasels, other, more aggressive gull species and humans to establish a new colony in Canada. To date they have returned every year, and in 1983, after four years of trying, they finally successfully raised two young. This small flock has provided scientists and conservationists with important lessons about what happens when a wildlife species tries to colonize a new area.

The bowhead whale, Eskimo curlew, pere-

grine falcon, Peary caribou, wolverine and Ross's and ivory gulls all demonstrate vividly the pressures on Arctic wildlife today. They are the symbols of what can happen to other wildlife if we do not protect their natural habitat by establishing reserves and if we do not avoid human disturbance and carefully control the numbers that are taken for human use.

Apart from special endangered species, there are many other conservation questions that must be addressed in the Arctic. We can't wait for more species to become endangered before we take steps to ensure their survival.

Polar bears are a good example, because Canada probably has half the world's population of this magnificent animal, regarded elsewhere as a threatened species. Polar bears are still hunted, under careful control, by the Inuit. But every year a further number are killed because they are "problem bears," maurauding oil exploration camps or villages.

We must make sure that the total killed each year is not so large that the population starts to decline. Furthermore, we are learning that polar bears can be grouped into subpopulations. Some of these subgroups, such as those in western Hudson Bay, appear to be healthy and reproducing well. Others, such as those in northern Quebec, may be in trouble. The problem, then, is not as simple as just monitoring polar bears in general; we must carefully define and watch the subpopulations.

Beluga whales are a similar case. Abundant in the western Arctic and western Hudson Bay, they are seriously depleted in eastern Hudson Bay, Ungava Bay and Cumberland Sound. Belugas spend eight to ten weeks of the summer in river estuaries, some of which are threatened by dredging, shipping, drilling, pollution, even hydroelectric dams further upstream.

Narwhals and walrus are examples of Arctic marine mammals that are heavily harvested by hunters despite there being no accurate estimate of how many there are. How can we be sure that the level of harvest is sustainable? The same question applies to proposals for capturing wild falcons for falconry.

Some of the great caribou herds also appear to have declined dramatically, in part because their migration routes have been bisected by roads or pipelines. Cooperative management committees have been established to allow native hunters and scientists to work together to make sure that too many caribou are not taken.

This trend towards cooperative research and management is a significant advance, for no person or group has a corner on wisdom when it comes to wildlife conservation in the Arctic. The native hunter can offer southern scientists valuable information based on generations of hunting experience and an all-season presence in the north. Good conservation work needs the guidance and observations that can be provided only by the Inuit. This cooperation is also beneficial because no effective enforcement of conservation measures in the Arctic is possible without agreement by the users that such controls are needed. It is not politically acceptable to arbitrarily impose quotas, nor is it practical given the size of the Arctic.

Native hunters can become an invaluable source of scientific information by reporting the occurrence of certain Arctic species and providing wildlife specimens. The World Wildlife Fund has already sought the help of native hunters and trappers on projects dealing with Arctic fox, caribou, narwhal, harp seals, ringed seals, polar bears, musk oxen, walrus, narwhal, beluga and bowhead whales. Many native hunters have expressed an interest in being trained to gather field information in a way that can be useful to scientists, which can include everything from measuring specimens to preparing field observations or harvest records.

Native land claims are not yet settled in the Arctic, and access to wildlife is a concern that has been consistently included in these claims. It is therefore unrealistic and insensitive, if not illegal, to propose management of northern game species without native involvement. Common sense and human decency dictate that those who have the greatest stake should have a say in the future of natural resources upon which they depend.

The beauty of our Arctic wilderness is envied by people from around the world. For this to be conserved requires cooperation between the north's people and others who care about it, good scientific fieldwork, complete assessment of the environmental impact of proposed industrial developments, and the protection of wildlife habitats through a system of parks, reserves and wilderness areas.

The Arctic may be a cold desert, but it is also a rich desert that pumps new life into the south while harboring the special creatures and people who live there year round. The Arctic is a world system, a place of importance, and its protection deserves the best efforts of mankind.

Photo Credits

Index